PORTAL KEY QUEST - VOLUME TWO

Ancient Ruins At The Depths Of The Bermuda Triangle

By

M.A. Joines

Copyright © 2011 M.A. Joines
All rights reserved.
ISBN: 0615547389
ISBN-13: 9780615547381
Library of Congress Control Number: 2011940254
M A Joines
Albany , OR

DEDICATION

I would like to dedicate this novel to my dear friend Kimberly Dickey. Your love and persistence encouraged me to explore options that until then I believed were not possible. Ultimately you gave me my most precious treasure and set me on the path to write these books.

CONTENTS

Chapter One	Pg 1
Chapter Two	Pg 5
Chapter Three	Pg 9
Chapter Four	Pg 13
Chapter Five	Pg 19
Chapter Six	Pg 27
Chapter Seven	Pg 31
Chapter Eight	Pg 37
Chapter Nine	Pg 45
Chapter Ten	Pg 51
Chapter Eleven	Pg 57
Chapter Twelve	Pg 61
Chapter Thirteen	Pg 69
Chapter Fourteen	Pg 75
Chapter Fifteen	Pg 83
Chapter Sixteen	Pg 89
Chapter Seventeen	Pg 95
Chapter Eighteen	Pg 99

Chapter 1

Aggie had been waiting in the sitting room for Professor Peabody and Lauren to return from their journey to Cairo. Ditty and Millie had cleared the tea service and biscuits hours ago, leaving Aggie alone with her cross-stitch and her thoughts. As she waited, the clock on the mantel began to chime. It was becoming increasingly difficult for her to be patient. She had important news to share with them, and it couldn't wait much longer. Suddenly the transport mechanism illuminated; someone had activated the device on Paradise Island.

"Finally," Aggie muttered, her agitated impatience shifting to relief. Professor Peabody and Lauren appeared next to the mantel clock just as it finished chiming. They had used the transport device REA had given them on Paradise Island.

"Oh, Grandma Aggie!" Lauren said as soon as she saw her. "We have so much to tell you!"

Aggie could contain herself no longer. She held up her hand to stop Lauren. "And I have much to tell you too, my dear. I must insist on going first as I have news of the upmost importance. While you were gone Lainey Elise activated her locator beacon. We've found her, and I'll need your help in recovering your twin sister."

"You found her, why that is amazing news!" Professor Peabody cried. "If she intentionally activated her locator beacon, then Lauren should be able to apperate directly to her energy signature. She must have recovered some or all of her memory." Then, turning to Lauren, he said, "I realize you must be weary considering we've just arrived home after a most satisfying, if not tiring, journey. I wonder, is it possible to ask that you indulge us just a bit longer before we call it a day?"

"If it means finding Lainey then I'll do whatever it takes," Lauren said firmly.

"I thought you might feel that way." Professor Peabody sounded pleased. "Well then, shall we hold hands?"

Lauren extended her hands to Professor Peabody and Grandma Aggie. She held on tightly as she closed her eyes and concentrated on her twin sister. Lainey and Lauren were as close as any set of twins could be. Knowing she was just about to see her sister again made Lauren's heart ache.

When she opened her eyes she immediately felt a wave of disappointment wash over her. They were still in the sitting room. Clearly Lainey had not recovered her memories. More than likely she had inadvertently activated the beacon, completely unaware of what she'd done.

"Well, that complicates things, doesn't it?" Aggie grumbled dismally, voicing what everyone felt. She turned to Professor Peabody. "What do you suggest we do now, Alistair? Lauren cannot apperate to someone whose memory has been compromised nor can she apperate to a location she has never seen before. According to the beacon, Lainey is deep within the wilderness well beyond paved roads. Although you and I are far from feeble, we certainly are in no condition to be traipsing through the rugged backwoods." She sighed heavily then said, "This is all very vexing. I need a sherry." Aggie moved to the server and poured herself and Professor Peabody a small glass of sherry. She handed him the glass and sat in her chair deep in thought.

The three of them sat quietly for a few moments trying desperately to figure out how to get to Lainey. Finally Lauren looked up and said, "Maybe we should ask REA."

"You think REA might be able to help us?" Professor Peabody inquired.

"I don't know," she said. "I hope so."

"It's worth a try," Professor Peabody said, standing up. The three of them moved to the mantel and Lauren activated the transport device. Five seconds later they were all standing next to the mantel in the sitting room on Paradise Island. The same spot they had left not more than ten minutes earlier.

"REA?" Aggie called.

"I am here," the smooth voice of REA answered.

"We have a dilemma we're hoping you can assist us with," Aggie said as she placed the receiver to the activator beacon on the coffee table. "This device shows the location of someone we desperately wish to find. Lauren has the ability to apperate, but only to a known location or energy signature. Unfortunately we have neither in this instance. Is there any way you can assist us?"

"Certainly," REA replied. Instantly a holographic image appeared above the beacon device showing the exact location of Lainey! Everyone gasped.

"Fascinating!" Professor Peabody remarked. "When was this image taken?"

"My retrieval of data is instantaneous. The image you are viewing is in what's known as *real time*," REA replied.

As if on cue, Lainey walked out of the door of the cabin in the hologram. She picked up the ax that lay beside a large stump and began chopping wood. The three of them watched, awestruck.

Chapter 2

"It is her!" Aggie croaked, nearly in tears. "Oh thank you, REA. You have been most helpful!"

"You are welcome," REA replied smoothly.

"Let's go!" Lauren said impatiently, extending her hands to Aggie and Professor Peabody.

"Lauren, we should probably apperate to a location hidden behind her. I don't want to run the risk of scaring her," Aggie said, regaining her composure. "I think once we arrive, you should make the initial contact since obviously you're her twin. The sight of you will be less startling."

"Okay," Lauren said and took Professor Peabody's and Aggie's hands eagerly. Holding tightly to their hands, she closed her eyes and concentrated on the image she'd just seen.
Before she opened her eyes she knew it had worked because the sound of chopping wood could be heard in the distance. Lauren opened her eyes and saw her twin sister for the first time since the portal gate accident. The group found themselves behind an enormous old growth pine tree that easily concealed all three of them. It was so massive that the top of the tree seemed to soar

well into the clouds above. Lainey was up ahead of them in a little clearing that let in huge shafts of sunlight. She looked tired and thin. She'd always been slim, but the time she'd spent in the woods had taken a toll on her. Her graceful, delicate facial features looked hard and chiseled on her tiny, thin frame. Her honey blonde hair was pulled back in a ponytail with a rubber band. Her beautiful, fair complexion was concealed beneath a layer of grime, but her strong, penetrating, nutmeg brown eyes were still there. They were Lauren's eyes.

Taking a deep breath, Lauren let go of Aggie's and Professor Peabody's hands and gave them a weak smile. Cautiously she emerged from her hiding place and slowly picked her way toward her twin sister. She moved as carefully as she could so as not to make a peep. Her mind was racing; she wasn't sure what she would say or what she would do when she finally looked into Lainey's eyes.

As she walked silently toward her sister she stumbled over a tree root and fell to the ground with a thump. Lainey spun around wildly with the ax raised above her head ready to defend herself against some rabid woodland beast. The expression on Lainey's face changed from alarm to curiosity as recognition registered. She lowered the ax and placed her hands on her hips as she watched Lauren awkwardly pick herself up off the ground and laugh weakly.

"Uh…hi," Lauren said, slightly embarrassed.
"Who are you?" Lainey asked suspiciously.

"Well, isn't it obvious? I'm your twin sister," Lauren said as she began to dust herself off. "And by the way, what were you intending to do with that ax?" she asked, a little annoyed but still embarrassed.

"I thought you were a bear!" Lainey said defensively.

"Have you seen any bears around here?" Lauren asked, her annoyance instantly changing to concern as she quickly scanned the woods.

"Well, not yet, but you never know," Lainey answered. Then a bit more apprehensively she asked, "How did you find me?"

"That's a long story, but suffice it to say we've been looking for you," Lauren answered truthfully.

"We?" Lainey asked. "Who's we?"

"Grandma Aggie, mostly, but all of us," Lauren said. "Do you remember anything?"

"No," Lainey said quietly. "Do you?"

"I do now, but not when I was found. Grandma Aggie came and got me. Once I was home the memory machine helped me recover my memories," Lauren answered.

Lainey was about to ask what she meant by "the memory machine" when she heard more rustling in the woods. She was just about to grab the ax again when she saw Grandma Aggie and Professor Peabody walking toward them. They were walking slowly so as to not frighten Lainey.

"Here's Professor Peabody and Grandma Aggie now," Lauren said, pointing them out.

"Where did they come from?" Lainey asked, startled and a little annoyed. "How many more are there?"

"I'll explain everything once we're home," Lauren said, chuckling.

"Oh my dear Lainey, I'm so relieved to have found you," Aggie said as she approached the girls. She held out her arms and took Lainey into a warm embrace. Lainey's initial reaction was to pull away, but then her fears seemed to melt away as she allowed herself to be held and comforted. She was surprised to feel tears stinging her eyes. She'd been so scared and alone when she woke up in the woods with no memory of who she was or how she'd gotten there. She had hiked for days with no idea of where she was. When she finally found the abandoned cabin it was like a life raft in the middle of an angry ocean. It may have been rustic, but at least she wasn't unprotected from the elements and she was able to stay dry at night. She learned to live off the land. She'd kept warm at night by the heat of a small woodstove inside the cabin. But she'd always hoped that somehow, someone was searching for her, that she had family who knew her and wanted her back home. She knew these people were her family. Even if she had no memory of them, she felt it in her soul. She trusted them.

"I think we're ready to go home now," Professor Peabody said quietly to Lauren.

Chapter 3

Lauren placed her arms around Lainey and Grandma Aggie as Professor Peabody placed his hand on her shoulder. She closed her eyes and concentrated on the sitting room. When she opened her eyes, they were home.

"How did we get here?" Lainey asked, startled and a little scared.

"It will be much easier to explain once your memories have been restored," Grandma Aggie responded.

"Okay," Lainey said, not quite convinced.

"Don't worry," Lauren said reassuringly. "I was scared too when I got home. Trust me; it's going to be alright. We all love you so very much and we're really happy you're home."

Lainey smiled at her gratefully, feeling a bit relieved.

"Come, dear," Aggie said as she took her hand and led her down the hall to the room that held the memory recovery system. "At first glance this may seem to be an ordinary table and chair, but in reality it's our memory recovery device. I won't get into the reasons why we have it, but suffice it to say its existence here has become extraordinarily useful. I'll ask that you take a seat in the chair and firmly grip the arms, please. That should activate the system."

Lainey did as she was asked. She slowly sat in the chair, unsure of what to expect. Then she carefully gripped the arms of the chair and held on.

Instantly a holographic globe appeared in the center of the table, and a blue light emanated from the sphere. The image was floating six inches above the table and filled the entire surface. A mechanical voice spoke. "Subject: Lainey Elise Wilkins. Memory corruption: 92.6 percent. Memory restoration: one hour, four minutes, twelve seconds. Proceed?"

Lainey looked stunned.

"Are you alright, dear?" Aggie asked.

"Yeah, I think so," Lainey replied.

"Do you need some time before you go on?" Aggie asked kindly. "You don't have to do anything you're not comfortable with, okay?"

"No, I'm ready," Lainey said more confidently.

"Very well," Aggie said. "To launch the program you'll need to give the command."

"Okay," Lainey said confidently. "Proceed."

Instantly images began flashing across the holographic screen. Lainey became transfixed. "I'll leave you in peace then," Aggie whispered as she quietly left the room. She went back to the sitting room where Professor Peabody and Lauren were waiting for her.

"I am so very grateful to both of you. Without your help I'm not certain how we would have found her," Aggie said wearily as she sat down. She hadn't realized just how tired she was until that moment. Aunt Ditty and Millie had come in with the tea service while Aggie was getting Lainey situated with the memory recovery device. Lauren poured Aggie a cup of tea and handed it to her. Aggie took it gratefully and gave Lauren's hand an affectionate squeeze.

"Tell me, dear, how was your adventure in Cairo?" Aggie asked.

Professor Peabody and Lauren excitedly shared their experience with everyone. They explained what happened when they arrived and how they met Professor Willhaus. They talked about the chamber and all the exquisite relics they'd seen. They also explained how Professor Willhaus had become instrumental in ultimately finding the hidden portal key.

The tea was exactly what they needed. Time to rest and refresh after their long journey to Cairo and then again to find Lainey. They hadn't realized that they'd been talking for over an hour until the door opened and Lainey came in. Everyone stopped and looked up as she entered the room. Lainey paused and scanned the room, resting her eyes on each person as she did so. Then she smiled and said, "Boy is it good to be home."

Lauren was the first to jump up. She threw her arms around her sister in a firm, affectionate embrace as tears welled in her eyes. "I missed you so much, Lainey," she croaked, unable to stop the tears now as they streamed freely down her cheeks. They had all missed Lainey desperately, but the bond between the twin sisters had always been exceptional. When Lauren finally let her sister go, Lainey hugged everyone else, happy beyond words that she was home.

"Lauren, why don't you and you sister head upstairs and get cleaned up before dinner? You both have had a most amazing day," Aggie said with a smile.

"Oh, dinner!" Lainey said. "Aunt Ditty, what have you made for dinner? I'm starved!"

"In honor of your return, I've made all your favorites," Aunt Ditty said, very pleased. "Pork roast with roasted potatoes, dilled carrots, and chocolate cake for dessert."

"Aunt Ditty, you are an ANGEL!" Lainey cried. "I've been eating nuts and berries for ages. Pork roast, oh, it sounds wonderful."

"Come on," Lauren said as she pulled her sister out of the sitting room and toward the stairs. "I need a long soak in a hot tub, and so do you! You smell like a lumberjack!"

"Hey! I've been living in the woods, you know!" Lainey protested as she followed her sister up the stairs.

Millie and Ditty sniggered as they started gathering the tea service. It was certainly wonderful to have the girls back, even if they did bicker.

Chapter 4

Lauren was on the bed combing out her long, honey brown hair as Lainey came out of the bathroom. Lainey had on a plush white robe that enveloped her, and her hair was wrapped in a thick white towel. Her checks were pink from the hot bath; she looked tired but very happy.

"Oh, that felt divine," Lainey said as she flopped down beside her sister on the bed and began filing her unruly nails.

"I know. I feel like I've washed off a week's worth of sand and grit," Lauren replied.

"You know, I still don't understand how we got back here," Lainey said casually.

"You're not going to believe this," Lauren said excitedly as she looked up. "I did it!"

Lainey stopped filing her nails and looked directly into Lauren's eyes. "You did it?" she asked, puzzled. "But how?"

"After Grandma Aggie found me and my memory was restored, I had a procedure done that redirects the neuro-electrical impulses in my brain. The device widens the pathways and allows me to access parts of my brain that have never been awakened before. In addition to higher intelligence I've also stimulated a region of my brain that holds special abilities. We all have hidden talents. Mine apparently is to apperate."

"That's incredible!" Lainey said, mesmerized.

"They always intended for us to choose the procedure when we were older, but because of the current situation they offered the option of doing this procedure now. After the portal gate collapsed it became imperative for us to explore the possibilities sooner."

"So if I have my neuro-electrical thingies widened too, I'll be able to apperate just like you?" Lainey asked excitedly.

"Uh...not exactly," Lauren said cautiously. "Everyone has different abilities. Your ability will be unique to you. You might be an apperater, but it could also be something different. Come on, we need to get dressed and head down to dinner. You know how Aunt Ditty gets if we're late!"

The girls began getting dressed for dinner. The only difference between them was their hair. Lauren kept hers long and pulled back with a head band while Lainey's hair was just past her shoulders and the sides were pulled up on top of her head and held there with a clip.

As they entered the dining room, they saw that the table had been set for a feast. Aunt Ditty was just putting the last dishes on the grand dining table.

"Oh, that smells so good!" Lainey said, breathing in the heavenly scent of pork roast with a caraway sage crust. Lainey and Lauren sat next to each other. In all the time they'd lived at Waverly Park, they had always been together. They had never been separated until the portal gate had scattered them like seeds in the wind. It wasn't hard to see how very much they had missed each other; the true bond of twins existed so strongly between them.

"I would like to offer a toast," Grandma Aggie said once everyone was seated. "To Lauren and Lainey—it is so very good to have you both home safe and sound. And may the rest of our lost loved ones return home quickly."

"Here! Here!" Everyone responded enthusiastically as they clinked glasses and drank deeply.

Dinner was as wonderful as anticipated, and Lainey had seconds of everything. The pork was succulent and tender with the edges crusty and flavorful. The potatoes were crisp and golden brown on the outside but tender and flakey on the inside. Sy had picked the carrots from the garden and Ditty had steamed them and tossed them with fresh dill. Of course there were warm rolls and a tossed salad to round off the meal. Everyone finished their meal and began chatting while they waited for Lainey to finish.

"There's one thing I still don't understand," Lauren said as they watched Lainey take one more roll and butter it. "How did you activate the locator beacon if you didn't have your memories?"

"Oh, yeah, I'd forgotten about that!" Lainey said between bites of hot buttered roll. "I was carrying a stack of firewood into the cabin. I had it balanced in my right arm as I reached the door handle. It was cold out and I didn't want to make two trips, so I overloaded myself a bit. At any rate, the top piece began to slip and I reached up with my left arm just as it came down and hit my wrist with full force. I yelped and dropped all the wood. I held my arm hoping I hadn't hurt it too bad. I remember feeling a crack. It didn't feel the way you'd expect a bone to feel if it was breaking. It wasn't a bone after all; turns out it was my locator beacon. Lucky, huh?"

"Lucky doesn't even begin to cover it," Aggie said with a smile.

Once Lainey had finally finished her dinner, they retired to the sitting room where they took their seats and contemplated having dessert—rich, luscious chocolate cake with a thick layer of chocolate butter cream frosting.

Before they began serving coffee and dessert, Professor Peabody turned to Lainey and said, "I know you've been through an amazing ordeal, but there is something we need to discuss with you."

"The neuro-pathway procedure?" Lainey asked.

"Why, yes," Professor Peabody said, taken aback.

"Lauren told me about it when we were upstairs. I know you wanted to wait until we were a bit older, but I understand why it's necessary to do it now," Lainey said.

"I see," Professor Peabody said. "I had forgotten that you girls talk about everything. This procedure should not be taken lightly. It might be a good idea to sleep on it. There are risks, you know."

"I understand about the risks. But I don't need to sleep on it. With most of our brothers and sisters still missing, I'd like to do it now if that's okay," Lainey stated firmly.

"You are very much like your sister—determined," Professor Peabody said, smiling. "Well then, I think we should head to my study. Lauren, you may come if you wish. I think Lainey could use your support."

Lainey gave Lauren a look that could only be described as pleading.

"I think I'd like to stay with Lainey," Lauren said.

Lainey smiled gratefully and held her sister's hand.

Chapter 5

The three of them left the sitting room and went to Professor Peabody's study. Once in the study, they made themselves comfortable while they waited for Professor Peabody to load his pipe and take a few satisfying puffs. Lainey nearly cried. It had been so long since she'd smelled the sweet smell of pipe tobacco. It smelled like home. Finally Professor Peabody put the pipe down and turned to Lainey.

"My dear, every individual, whether from Earth or Althus, has abilities that may be considered a gift or magic by uneducated minds. It is not extraordinary once you understand that every human being is born with these special talents. Earth humans just have not learned to access that knowledge yet. That is what we intend to rectify for you tonight. Most individuals master one form of extraordinary manipulation. Aggie is more advanced than most. She has mastered a few skills, specifically time manipulation and memory control. My skill is phasing, and your sister is able to apperate. You, my dear, have not had the pleasure of exploring your skill. We shall now give you the tools you need to access that part of your brain which has not yet been explored. Before we begin, you must know that we have a responsibility to ourselves and our fellow human beings—from Earth or elsewhere—to use our gifts in only kindness and compassion. We never use our gifts for selfish or sinister intent. Is that clear?"

"I understand," Lainey said firmly.

Professor Peabody smiled. "Very well, I shall explain everything that I am about to do," he said as walked to the locked credenza behind his desk. He took out an ancient looking box and placed it on his desk. He carefully unlatched the box and opened it. Inside was what looked like a plum-colored velvet pillow. Nestled in the middle was an instrument that fit easily in one hand. It narrowed a bit at the top. Professor Peabody lifted the device from its resting place and walked over to Lainey.

"This instrument is used to redirect neuro-electrical impulses in your brain as well as widen the pathways," he said. "It is placed in your left ear if you are right-handed or your right ear if you are left-handed. The procedure is painless and takes but a few seconds to complete. I ask that you try to remain as still as possible while we perform this procedure. Once the procedure is complete I will ask you some simple questions to ensure that it was a success. Once we have established that, then I will leave you to your thoughts for a little while. That should give you enough time to explore the changes that have occurred in your mind. Now then, you are right-handed, are you not?"

"Yes," Lainey replied.

"Very good, are you prepared to proceed?" he asked.

"Yes," Lainey said nervously and glanced at Lauren with a weak smile. Lauren returned the smile and gave Lainey a confident nod.

"Fine, please sit quietly while I place the device in your ear," he said, and with that he gently placed the instrument in Lainey's left ear. She closed her eyes and took a deep breath. As Professor Peabody activated the neuro-pathway device, a green light glowed from the tip, emitting a pulse for a few seconds, and then the glowing ended. He gently removed the instrument from her ear as her eyes fluttered open.

"Holy smokes!" she said, amazed.

He chuckled. "Yes, your sister had a similar reaction. Now I must ask you: What is your name?"

"Lainey Elise Wilkins," Lainey replied.

"Good. And where are we?

"Waverly Park Subterrania."

"Fine, and who is that?"

"My sister Lauren," she said, smiling.

Professor Peabody said with a satisfied smile, "Nicely done. Everything seems in order. Do you need a moment to gather your thoughts?" he asked as he turned back to the desk to return the device to the box. He carefully closed the lid and slid it back into its home in the credenza.

"I think I'd rather just finish what we're doing. Then I can spend some time exploring with Lauren," Lainey said.

"Fair enough, then we shall begin to investigate the part of your mind you have not had the pleasure of exploring before. You should now be able to access the special gift that you were born with. Please sit comfortably in your chair and close your eyes."

Lainey sat cross-legged on the sofa and closed her eyes.

"Good. Now take a few deep breaths and allow your mind to begin focusing. There is a sense that will start to overtake you. Do not fear it; allow it to freely engulf you." Professor Peabody observed her carefully as he spoke. He watched her face. It was tranquil and serene. Suddenly he saw the change come over her. He knew at that moment she had found the location in her mind that held her secret attribute. He watched her intently. The first experience could be a bit tricky, mostly because the subject didn't know what to expect. He noticed the slightest edge of a force field appear around her.

"Excellent!" he cried. "If I'm not mistaken, your hidden attribute is a force field."

"A force field?" Lainey asked, unable to conceal her disappointment. "Why did Lauren get something neat like apperating and I get stuck with a crummy old force field?"

"You do not believe a force field would be a useful attribute?" Professor Peabody asked with a raised eyebrow.

"No! I don't," Lainey said obstinately as a bit of self-pity began to creep into her tone. "Lauren can pop in and out, and that's really neat. How is putting up a force field neat?"

Without responding, Professor Peabody picked up a dictionary from his desk and threw it directly at Lainey's head.

"Hey!" Lainey yelped as she threw her arms up to block the book from impacting her head.

Lauren watched in horror as the whole event unfolded. She couldn't wrap her mind around what was happening. But the instant Lainey realized the book was headed in her direction she instinctively put up her force field. The book slammed into the edge of the force field and dropped to the floor like a stone. It took a moment for the full impact of what had just occurred to register with Lauren.

"Oh! That's cool!" Lauren said, impressed.

"It didn't hit me?" Lainey asked a bit confused.

"No. It did not hit you," Professor Peabody said. "Your force field is now a part of you. It has become an automatic reflex just as breathing and blinking are. The challenge for you will be to learn how to control it. Lauren can either apperate or not, there is no middle ground with her gift. You, on the other hand, need to learn how to draw on it and be in command of it."

There was a sudden commotion at the door and Grandma Aggie, Aunt Ditty, and Aunt Millie came bursting in.

"We heard a scream and then a thud!" Millie said urgently. "Is everything alright?"

"Sorry," Lainey said sheepishly. "That was me."

"I was demonstrating to Lainey just how useful her gift can be. You see, she has the ability to create a force field."

"Really!" Grandma Aggie said, impressed. "It seems that you and your sister have very uncommon attributes indeed."

Lainey seemed happy to hear that, and her spirits picked up a bit. "So it's not a very common gift?" she asked, feeling a little less disappointed. "I'm just not sure what use it will be, though."

"No?" Grandma Aggie asked as she raised one eyebrow. "Well, let me see if we can enlighten you. Correct me if I'm mistaken, Professor Peabody, but I believe that Lainey now has the ability to visit any atmosphere without suffering ill effects. Let me explain. You can now spend as much time as you like in locations that would be considered, at the very least, inhospitable to most and at the very worst, lethal. Your force field will provide you with a comfortable ambient air temperature of 74 degrees and humidity of 50 percent with an inextinguishable supply of breathable oxygen."

"Grandma Aggie is absolutely right," Professor Peabody agreed. "You can be at the icy depths of the bottom of the ocean or within the unimaginable heat of a lava flow and feel no ill effects. You also have the ability to push your force field out to encompass anyone in your party or any structure. With Lauren's gift there must be physical contact, but your gift is not limited by those restrictions. It really is quite remarkable."

Lainey sat a little taller and a grin began to sneak across her face. "Force field, huh?" she said, feeling a bit more pleased with herself.

"Oh! I just remembered the quest for the portal key!" Lauren said to Professor Peabody impatiently. "Lainey is the missing piece to the puzzle! We needed someone who possesses the skill of force fields. Now we can recover the portal key!" she said excitedly.

"Hold on," he said. "Not so fast! Lainey has a lot of work ahead of her before she can participate in this quest. She needs to be in absolute control of her ability before we can go forward with this expedition. Remember it's at the bottom of the ocean, and she will need to hold her force field and push it out to encompass the crystal pyramid. If her force field fails while we are down there..." His voice trailed off.

"...We could die." Lauren finished his thought somberly, fully grasping the severity of the situation.

Lainey's eyes grew wide. "I'm not ready for that yet! I need to practice first, Lauren!" she said in a shaky voice as panic engulfed her.

Aunt Ditty realized Lainey was going to cry, so she put her hand on her shoulder. "There's nothing more that can be done this evening then. Let's all have some cake and a nice cup of coffee. Come on, dear, up you go."

Once everyone was back in the sitting room and the coffee and cake had been served, the conversation became lively and pleasant again. Sy continued to complain about the bunnies eating his vegetables and Millie kept trying to get Lainey to eat more cake. Professor Peabody and Lauren told stories about their adventures in Cairo and about their new friend, Professor Willhaus.

Chapter 6

As the evening drew on and the clock chimed ten, Grandma Aggie said it was time for bed. Usually Lauren and Lainey protested, but tonight the girls welcomed it. It had been an exhausting day for Lainey and an extraordinarily long day for Professor Peabody and Lauren. They climbed the stairs together, followed by Bowser and Bosco, the Boston terriers. Their rooms were beside each other, connected by a "Jack and Jill" bathroom. As much as Bosco was Lauren's boy, so Bowser was Lainey's. All dogs have a strong attachment to a certain person that they are most fond of. Lainey was Bowser's special someone, and Boston terriers take that attachment to a new level as they give their entire heart to their chosen one. Bowser had a very tiny twisted little tail that, when he wagged, caused his whole back side to wiggle. He was having a hard time tonight because every time Lainey looked at him and smiled, he wiggled like crazy.

Typically the girls would stay up late and chat, but tonight they both wanted nothing more than to climb into their own warm beds, with their crisp, clean sheets, thick comforters, and downy pillows. Lauren had to move Bosco over to get into bed. He dove under the covers, did three circles at the foot of the bed, and went out cold. Lauren wasn't far behind him.

Lainey, on the other hand, crawled into bed with Bowser nestled right beside her. She nuzzled up next to him and took a deep breath—he smelled like home. Tears stung her eyes. She was home. No more cold, damp nights in that rickety old cabin. No more hungry mornings foraging for food. The crisp, clean sheets felt like heaven to her. Bowser began to snore loudly and she laughed out loud. She kissed his head and snuggled deeper into her pillow. She was asleep moments later.

The next morning the girls arrived at breakfast together with Bowser and Bosco trotting closely behind them. Aunt Ditty had made biscuits and sausage gravy, scrambled eggs, and the ever present orange juice and fruit salad. Grandma Aggie was sipping her coffee when they arrived.

"Ah, ladies!" she said. "I trust that you slept well."

"I haven't slept that well in ages," Lainey said happily as she broke open a fat, fluffy biscuit then poured a huge spoonful of gravy over it. "I was so grateful to find that little cabin after being lost in the woods, but that was nothing compared to how I felt when I crawled into my own bed last night. My own, warm bed with Bowser by my side, snoring. I was safe, my tummy was full, and I was warm."

Aunt Ditty made some comment about something in her eye as she dabbed tears with her napkin, and Sy cleared his throat and got up pretending he needed something else from the buffet. Grandma Aggie was quiet for a moment as she stared into her cup of coffee. Lainey and Lauren sat down with their plates loaded with food.

"Was that you snoring last night?" Lauren asked Lainey.

"NO!" Lainey replied, slightly offended. Everyone laughed, grateful for the diversion. "Bowser has always snored," Lainey continued. "It used to wake me up at times, but it's like a lullaby to me now."

Professor Peabody turned to Lauren and Lainey. "I've come up with an idea that I believe will help Lainey learn to control her powers," he said. "How about after breakfast we head to the lake and do some control work?"

"That sounds good to me," Lauren said. Lainey just nodded and mumbled because she had just taken a bite of her breakfast. They had a nice, relaxing breakfast. Everyone sat around sipping coffee after they were finished. Lainey seemed to be making up for lost time. She mounded her plate twice with biscuits and gravy. Finally when she said she couldn't eat another bite, they headed upstairs to get ready for the control work Professor Peabody had mentioned.

Chapter 7

The sun was high in the sky when they left the sitting room through the French doors. The forest across the lake was showing the unmistakable signs of autumn. Leaves were beginning to change color and there was a crispness in the air. Soon summer would be a memory and winter would be hard on their heels. Professor Peabody was leaning against the low fence surrounding the vegetable garden as he smoked his pipe. He was chatting with Sy who was harvesting his crop of carrots and beets. There were still stragglers on the tomato bushes, but the cold weather had slowed the production of new fruit. The far side of the garden had fat pumpkins and butternut and acorn squash that would be harvested in the next few weeks or so. The potatoes were ready too. Soon the garden would be a memory and the cellar would be filled with root vegetables that would last through winter.

Lauren snapped an apple off the tree and took a crunchy bite. It was sweet and tart and juicy. Ditty would be making apple pie filling soon and the whole house would smell of cooked apples and cinnamon. The thought made her heart happy. As they got closer to the garden they smiled as they heard Sy complaining about the rabbits eating his carrots. Sy always complained about the rabbits eating his carrots. Apparently the fence he'd placed around the garden wasn't a deterrent because the bunnies just dug underneath it, much to his annoyance.

"Ah, ladies," Professor Peabody greeted them as they arrived. "Are you ready for our lesson?"

"Sure," Lainey said unconcerned.

"Bunnies again?" Lauren asked Sy sympathetically.

"Ugh, the little varmints!" Sy complained bitterly, which just annoyed him all over again.

"Well then, shall we head down to the dock?" Professor Peabody motioned toward the lake. They left Sy muttering in the garden and headed down the path toward the lake. As they walked by the lake's edge the swans eyed them suspiciously. The girls were happy they'd put on turtlenecks and warm sweaters because the air was crisp and a slight breeze had begun to blow the orange and pink leaves around. Soon fall would be gone and winter would come and dust everything in a blanket of thick, white snow.

"Alright, here is what I would like you to do," Professor Peabody started when they arrived at the dock. "Lainey, begin concentrating on your force field, allowing it to encompass Lauren. Hold hands and jump into the lake."

At first they just stared at him until they realized he was serious.

"You're kidding, right?" Lainey asked incredulously.

"Oh, I am perfectly serious," he replied. "If all goes well, you should remain quite dry."

The girls looked at each other, shrugged their shoulders, and then held hands. Lainey began to concentrate, and her force field appeared around them both.

"Cool," Lauren whispered softly. Holding hands, they leapt from the dock toward the water. Surprisingly the force field acted like a bubble as they floated on the surface.

"Well, that was unexpected," Professor Peabody said, surprised. He had expected them to sink below the surface of the water, not float on top like a bubble. But as he spoke those words, Lainey glanced at him, breaking her concentration and causing the force field to collapse. The girls shrieked and dropped into the lake like stones disappearing from sight. Instantly they resurfaced, sputtering and soaking wet.

"LAINEY!" Lauren hissed, annoyed.

"Sorry," Lainey said sheepishly. "I got distracted."

They slogged back to the dock and heaved themselves out of the lake as Professor Peabody tried unsuccessfully to conceal his amusement. They stood dripping wet and soaked to the bone.

"Again, please," he said with authority.

They stared at him with mouths agape.

"We're soaked!" Lauren said incredulously.

"...And freezing!" Lainey chimed in.

"Then you will not mind if it happens again," he said calmly. "Shall we? Alright, Lainey, concentrate."

Reluctantly Lainey began to concentrate once more, causing her force field to reappear, but this time it seemed stronger somehow. She felt more in control of it, as if she didn't have to focus as hard. The girls held hands and leapt off the dock for the second time that morning. They floated on the water just as they had the first time. They weren't cold anymore because inside Lainey's force field it was warm and cozy. Lauren let go of her sister's hand and placed both hands on the edge of the force field. It felt solid and safe, as if it were a wall. She leaned on it but it didn't move. She jumped up and down but still it didn't move. Lainey's force field held strong. They were unaware that behind them Professor Peabody had picked up a large rock. He hefted the rock off the edge of the dock. It made a loud, deep, THUNK sound. There was an enormous splash with large rippling wakes of water fanning outward toward the girls. Lauren and Lainey gasped simultaneously and swung around, but the force field held. They continued to bob on the surface of the water as the wakes passed under the force field.

"Well done, Lainey," Professor Peabody said with a grin. "You seem to be gaining control of your ability. I think that should do it for today. Lauren, would you apperate your sister and yourself back to the dock, please?"

Lauren took Lainey's hand and instantly they were back on the dock as Lainey dropped her force field.

"We shall try again tomorrow," Professor Peabody said. "Now I think we should head back to the house and get you two dried off."

Considering they were cold and wet, the girls seemed in very good spirits. Lainey had managed to strengthen her force field enough that it held when she was startled. That was certainly progress.

The next day went much better. Lainey was able to control her ability with much less effort and seemed to have a better understanding of it. Much to the girls' relief, they did not end up in the lake again. Over the next few weeks they continued to practice. The days were getting shorter and the weather was turning cold. Lainey's abilities strengthened each day until she knew, without a shadow of a doubt, that she had absolute control over her ability.

Chapter 8

"I'm ready," Lainey said one morning over breakfast.

"For what, more breakfast?" Lauren asked dryly.

"No," Lainey said, resisting the urge to roll her eyes, "for the quest."

"Are you certain?" Professor Peabody asked, surprised, his fork frozen mid-air between his mouth and the plate full of French toast.

"I am," she replied confidently. "You're the one that said I'd know when it was time. It's time! I feel it. I know it. It's like a part of me now. When my ability first appeared, it felt foreign, like a tight pair of shoes, but now that I've worked it, it's become comfortable and familiar. Surprisingly I don't know what I'd do without it. It's really hard to explain."

"You feel confident then that you are ready for the quest?" he asked again. "You understand that our lives will be in your hands. Are you comfortable with that?"

When she first realized what her gift was she had been gripped with fear. She had no confidence in her ability and certainly didn't want the responsibility of keeping others safe, particularly on the quest. But since then, over the past few weeks, she had worked her skill as if it were a muscle. Every time she used the force field she grew more sure of herself, more certain of her abilities. Now she knew in all certainty that she could and would keep them safe.

"I can keep us safe, I know I can," Lainey finally answered confidently.

Professor Peabody put his fork down and smiled at her. "Splendid!" he exclaimed. "I have felt for some time that you were ready, but you could not gain control until you felt the shift in the balance of power. That balance between fear and control. Once your mind achieved the confidence needed, then your ability was mastered."

"It's true!" Lainey marveled. "I knew my ability was getting stronger. Every time I used my force field the fear would be weaker. It began to fade until it disappeared completely. I didn't even notice it was gone until I thought about it last night as I was drifting off to sleep."

"I am so very proud of you, Lainey," Professor Peabody beamed. "I believe we should give our old friend Professor Willhaus a visit."

Lainey looked confused but Lauren was delighted.

Professor Peabody and the girls met back in the sitting room after breakfast. They wanted to catch Professor Willhaus before he left his library.

They were finally ready to start the next quest. Grandma Aggie was there to see them off.

"Please be careful," Aggie said, trying to keep the concern from her tone.

"We will, Gran," Lauren said and kissed her lightly on the cheek. "Love you!"

"We should get going; I would like to catch Reggie before he leaves his library."

Lauren held Lainey's and Professor Peabody's hands. She smiled at Grandma Aggie one last time, then closed her eyes and concentrated on Professor Willhaus' energy signature. Before Lauren opened her eyes she knew they'd arrived because she heard an audible gasp that she suspected came from Professor Willhaus.

"I don't think I'll ever get used to that!" Professor Willhaus said in exasperation as he stood up.

"Sorry, old chap," Professor Peabody said, slightly amused.

"Alistair!" Professor Willhaus said warmly as he shook Professor Peabody's hand. "It's so good to see you again."

"You too, Reggie," Professor Peabody replied.

"And Lauren, you're just as lovely as ever," Professor Willhaus said, smiling.

"Um, I'm not Lauren. I'm Lainey," Lainey said truthfully.

Professor Willhaus stopped in his tracks with a look of confusion on his face.

"I'm Lauren," Lauren said from behind him.

He spun around to see Lauren wiggling the tips of her fingers in a little wave. He looked from one to the other, dumbfounded.

"I didn't know you had a twin!" Professor Willhaus said to Lauren. "Fascinating!" Then to Lainey he said, "Well, it's lovely to meet you, my dear, and do you have a special gift as well?"

"Yes, I do. I have a force field," Lainey said proudly.

"A force field. Remarkable!" Professor Willhaus replied. He was captivated and clearly intended to discuss the matter in depth. Professor Peabody saw the look in his friend's eyes and knew that they were about to lose the afternoon if he didn't change the subject quickly.

"Reggie, I wonder if we could trouble you on another matter?" Professor Peabody asked quickly. "You were so helpful with our previous quest, and we were hoping you could assist us again on this one as well."

Professor Willhaus reluctantly drew his attention away from Lainey. "Of course, Alistair," he replied. "Where is the 'portal key' hidden this time?"

"Atlantis," Professor Peabody stated. "The crystal pyramid, to be exact, near the Tongue of the Ocean."

"Atlantis!" Professor Willhaus said excitedly, his whole demeanor changed. He clapped his hands and enthusiastically rubbed them together as all thoughts of exploring Lainey's abilities further vanished with that one word, *Atlantis*. "Now you have my full attention! I would be happy to impart my knowledge of this fascinating subject to you." Then he stopped and began looking around his library. "However, I believe this room may be a bit uncomfortable for an afternoon of lecturing," he said, a bit concerned as he began moving books off of chairs and eyeing the layer of dust on the table.

"Not to worry, my friend. I think we might be more comfortable at Waverly Park. Ditty would be happy to have a fresh face at her luncheon today, and we could have all the privacy we need to discuss this subject at length without censuring ourselves," Professor Peabody said with a wink.

Professor Willhaus could hardly contain his excitement. "Waverly Park! Oh...I just need to grab my laptop..." He scurried about his office. "...Ready!" he said breathlessly.

Lauren and Lainey did their best not to giggle.

"Splendid," Professor Peabody said, then to Lauren, "Shall we, my dear?"

Lauren held out her hands to Lainey and Professor Willhaus while Professor Peabody placed his hand on her shoulder. She closed her eyes and concentrated on the sitting room back home. When she opened her eyes she saw they had returned home. Professor Willhaus was in awe as he surveyed his new surroundings with delight.

"Would you girls please tell Aunt Ditty that we will be having a guest joining us for lunch and most likely dinner as well," Professor Peabody said. "I shall take this opportunity to show Reggie around and introduce him to everyone. We should probably have lunch first. I find thinking is always easier on a full stomach. Then we shall get to work. Sound good?" Everyone agreed, and the girls left to find Ditty.

"Alistair, this is amazing!" Professor Willhaus said. "All of this is underground? It's positively unbelievable! It seems just as light and bright as if we were above ground. How is that possible?"

"Our world exists in a void beneath the trees," Professor Peabody explained. "As high as the trees are tall is how deep the void beneath the roots is. The canopy of the trees acts as a conduit. Our atmosphere is a mirror image of what is taking place above us. When it snows above us, we have snow here as well. When it is summer above, it is summer below. Our air is pure and clean because it is provided by the trees. It really is quite comfortable."

"Amazing!" Professor Willhaus exclaimed.

Professor Peabody and Professor Willhaus began walking toward the door when Aggie walked in.

"Oh!" Aggie gasped.

"Aggie, I would like to introduce Professor Reginald Willhaus. Reggie, this is Agatha Connelly," Professor Peabody said.

"I'm very pleased to meet you, sir," Aggie said as she extended her hand to shake Professor Willhaus'. "If I'm not mistaken I believe we owe you a great debt of gratitude. As I understand it, you were instrumental in finding the hidden chamber beneath the Great Sphinx. I welcome you into our home and hope you enjoy your stay with us."

Professor Willhaus took Aggie's hand and said, "I believe I'm the one who should be thanking you. My life has become quite dull in recent years. There is nothing like being put out to pasture to make one feel obsolete. No, I'm exceedingly grateful for the opportunity to offer my assistance. Indeed I find the company inspiring and motivating."

"Well then, we're happy to have you," Aggie said, pleased.

"I thought I'd show the old chap around before luncheon," Professor Peabody said to Aggie.

"Yes, that's a fine idea," Aggie said. "Have you spoken to Ditty yet? You know how she is about this sort of thing."

"Yes. The girls left just before you arrived. I should think everything is in order," Professor Peabody said.

"Very good, I'll leave you boys to it then," Aggie said, smiling. Professor Peabody and Professor Willhaus both bowed and left the room.

Aggie sniggered and thought to herself, *Two peas in a pod.*

Chapter 9

Professor Willhaus was sure that he had never been happier as he sat at the lunch table eating his meal with such enjoyable company. For the first course they had an amazing chicken noodle soup with crusty bread. Then came the spinach quiche, which was cooked to perfection, followed by a fresh garden salad. The conversation was pleasant, and he felt completely at home with these people. No pretences or agendas here. *How refreshing*, he thought. Millie sat next to him and he found her to be delightful company.

"Ditty, you have outdone yourself this time!" Professor Peabody exclaimed. "Lunch was wonderful, but now I believe it's time to get to work." Then he turned to Professor Willhaus and the girls. "Shall we retire to the library?"

"Yes, of course," Professor Willhaus said, placing his napkin on the table. "But first I must compliment you, madam, on a most satisfying meal, simply delightful!"

"Why, thank you, sir," Ditty said, smiling.

"I'll bring tea to the library in a bit then?" Millie asked Professor Peabody.

"Oh, Millie dear, that would be very kind of you," Professor Peabody replied.

The two professors stood, and Professor Peabody turned back to Lauren and Lainey. "Can I assume you two will be joining us?"

"We'll be right there," Lainey called to them as they left the dining room. "Ready?" she whispered to her sister.

"What are you girls up to?" Aggie asked with a wry grin.

"We're just practicing," Lauren said, trying to sound sincere.

"Let's go!" Lainey whispered a bit more urgently.

"Okay," Lauren said as she took her sister's hand and began concentrating on the library. Instantly they vanished from the dining room.

"Stinkers!" Aggie said with a smile.

Lauren and Lainey arrived at the library just before Professor Peabody and Professor Willhaus arrived. They could hear them talking as they came down the hall. They opened the door and were startled to see the girls already there.

"What took you so long?" Lainey asked innocently, suppressing a giggle.

"Some of us must travel the old-fashioned way, it is called walking!" Professor Peabody replied in a jesting tone. "Well, since we're all here, shall we find our seats and get comfortable? I'm extraordinarily interested in what Professor Willhaus has to share with us."

"I think you will find this topic as interesting or perhaps even more so than the information

ANCIENT RUINS AT THE DEPTHS OF THE BERMUDA TRIANGLE

I shared with you about the Great Sphinx," Professor Willhaus began. "Atlantis is one of the great mysteries of this world. True evidence of its existence began to surface in the 1970s. Naturally the scientific community shunned these discoveries, considering them to be hoaxes. One of the most compelling accounts was made by a credible physician who found undisputable evidence while scuba diving near the Bahamas in 1970. It's said that while he was diving he became separated from his companions. As he searched to rejoin his group he came upon a large structure looming ahead of him. As he drew closer he recognized it to be a pyramid. However, it was not a traditional pyramid made of stone, but one made of crystal. He had found a crystal pyramid!" he proclaimed, wide-eyed. "The doctor estimated that the pyramid was nearly forty fathoms deep and…"

"Excuse me, Professor Willhaus," Lauren interrupted, "but what exactly is a *fathom*?"

"Oh, brilliant question, my dear," Professor Willhaus answered happily. "A fathom is an old nautical or sailor's form of measurement. A fathom is equal to the depth of approximately six feet."

"That would make it…240 feet deep!" Lainey said, doing quick math in her head.

"Well done, Lainey!" Professor Willhaus said. "Yes, it's certainly hidden deep beneath the surface. At any rate, the doctor estimated that the pyramid was nearly forty fathoms deep and over 120 feet high with approximately thirty feet of its foundation buried beneath the sea floor. The exterior was constructed entirely of crystal blocks, and the surface was smooth and shiny like a mirror with the joints so exact that they were nearly indiscernible."

"Was this near the Tongue of the Ocean?" Professor Peabody asked.

"Yes, it was," Professor Willhaus answered. "Approximately twenty miles from the drop-off, as I understand it.

"This must be the same pyramid we're looking for then," Lauren said excitedly.

"Intriguing," Professor Willhaus pondered. "Well, it seems that the good doctor swam around the structure for a while searching for an opening when he managed to find an entrance at the capstone. He made his way through a passageway until he came to a room with a pyramid-shaped ceiling. Remarkably the room had no signs of sea life as one would expect of a structure at the bottom of the ocean. It is not uncommon for coral or fish to take up residence in a sunken vessel almost immediately, yet this structure was pristine on the inside. Curious indeed!

"The doctor stated that he was able to see perfectly and that the room was well lit. It is understandable that light can penetrate crystal, but not at the depths he suggested. I believe it is self-illuminating, just as we found the hidden chamber in Egypt to be. He described the interior room as some sort of electrical conducting chamber. There was a brassy type of metallic rod approximately three inches in diameter suspended from the uppermost point in the ceiling. Attached at the tip was a large red gem, which came to a point directly over a set of life-sized hands that appeared to be made of bronze and situated on an altar of stone. The hands had been charred and blackened as if tremendous current had burned them. Nestled in the hands was a crystal sphere nearly four inches in diameter. It is said that when the doctor left, he took the crystal sphere with him. Just what purpose the crystal sphere had remains a mystery. Some have concluded that the crystal sphere holds great volumes of knowledge, while others believe its purpose was to conduct vast amounts of energy. Either theory is possible considering how little we know about crystals and crystal technology." Professor Willhaus paused, deep in thought.

"It's interesting to note that the crystal pyramid, located near the Tongue of the Ocean, happens to be within the mythical Bermuda Triangle. There have been countless instances of ships and aircraft mysteriously vanishing within that triangulation. Apparently all contact with the vessel is lost and it subsequently disappears completely, never to be heard from again! I find it fascinating that the sunken ruins of Atlantis exist within the exact location of the Bermuda Triangle. Theories suggest that the Atlantians used those crystal pyramids as a sort of energy system or power grid. It would not be difficult to imagine, considering the Atlantians' advanced technology, that those crystal pyramids could actually still be functional. If that's the case then perhaps they are still energized and periodically vent energy, causing anomalies such as dematerialization of various craft in the vicinity at the time. Those ships and airplanes might just have been in the wrong place at the wrong time."

The happy group spent the better part of the afternoon drinking tea and discussing Atlantis, the crystal pyramids, and making arrangements to retrieve the portal key.

Chapter 10

There was a knock at the door.

"Come in!" Professor Peabody called.

The door opened and Millie appeared. "I hope you're ready for supper. Ditty's made a fine feast for us tonight," Millie said.

"I had not realized how hungry I had become until this very moment," Professor Peabody said as he stood up. "Will you girls be accompanying us or shall we meet you there?" he asked with a light-hearted smirk.

Lauren and Lainey just giggled as the two professors and Millie left the study. As expected, they arrived in the dining room before the others. Ditty was placing the last dishes of the feast on the server. Tonight's meal consisted of a mountain of crispy fried chicken, mashed potatoes with gravy, coleslaw, corn-on-the-cob, and fluffy hot biscuits.

"Oh, Aunt Ditty, this looks wonderful," Lainey said as she reached across the server for a biscuit.

Exasperated, Ditty placed her hands on her hips and gave Lainey a stern look. "First of all, little missy, you'll not be stealing any more biscuits until dinner, and second, you scare the dickens out of me every time you and your sister *pop in* like that!"

Lainey took another bite of the warm, tender biscuit and smiled mischievously. She then pecked Ditty on the cheek and took her seat, completely unaffected by the scolding. Ditty's expression softened as she tried to hold back a grin. She had missed those girls something fierce. Making things that filled their tummies and nurtured their souls was one of her greatest pleasures. It was Ditty's gift, just as phasing was Professor Peabody's. She had fed them when they were babies, and every meal that they took came from her heart. Cooking never felt like a chore to her because she loved them so much.

She thought about the other children that were still missing and her heart ached. Who was feeding them? Were their tummies empty? When would they be home? She was on the verge of tears when Professor Peabody, Professor Willhaus, and Millie came through the door. Relieved, she busied herself with the final preparation for dinner as she quickly dried her eyes. *The others will be home soon, and then what a feast we'll have,* she thought.

Dinner was just as wonderful as they had imagined. The chicken was crispy on the outside but juicy and tender on the inside. The mashed potatoes were light and fluffy but also creamy and rich, perfect by themselves but better with a generous helping of gravy cascading down the sides. The coleslaw was sweet and tangy with the right amount of crunch in a creamy sauce.

"I can't remember the last time I've had such delicious fried chicken," Professor Willhaus said, "and your mashed potatoes are superb."

"Then have a bit more, Professor," Ditty said as she handed him the bowl.

"Thank you, I think I shall," Professor Willhaus said, "...and please, call me Reggie."

"I'll take that bowl from you when you're finished," Lainey said, still making up for lost time. She didn't need gravy for Aunt Ditty's mashed potatoes. She just put a mound of butter on top and let it melt down the sides in little rivulets. The gravy she saved for dipping her biscuit. Lauren just watched her sister in amazement and wondered where she put it all. Lainey was just as slim as ever.

When they finally finished dinner they retired to the sitting room. Once everyone was settled, Ditty brought in the coffee and dessert. Tonight she had made a warm berry crisp and served it over vanilla ice cream. The combination of hot berries over cold ice cream is one of life's greatest pleasures.

"I think we should attempt to retrieve the portal key tomorrow after breakfast," Professor Peabody suggested. "Reggie, if it's not terribly inconvenient, would you be willing to accompany us on this expedition as well?"

"Why, I'd be delighted!" Professor Willhaus replied enthusiastically.

"Brilliant!" Professor Peabody cried. "Your insight is most appreciated."

"Well then, it would only make sense that you should stay here with us tonight," Aggie said, stating the obvious.

"I'd better get a room ready for you then!" Millie said as she stood up.

"I think you'll be needing some clothes as well," Ditty said to Professor Willhaus. "I'd better go with you, Millie."

"Please, ladies, don't go to any trouble on my account," Professor Willhaus protested.

"It's no trouble at all," Millie said honestly. "We'll just be a moment." And they both bustled out of the sitting room.

"Professor Willhaus, if you intend to join this expedition I think it wise that you be fitted with a locator beacon," Aggie said. "It's completely up to you; however we consider it a necessity and each of us has one."

"What exactly is a locator beacon?" he asked.

"A locator beacon is a tiny device, no larger than a grain of rice, which is positioned on the inside of your wrist. It's almost indiscernible once placed," Professor Peabody explained. "However, if for any reason you become separated from our party it can easily be activated by breaking the device. A distress signal will trigger here and your exact location will be identified and tracked. It would make finding and returning you to safety much easier. But to be clear, your location is only apparent when the device is activated. We cannot, nor are we interested in, tracking you or your movements. Once implanted the device is inert and remains so until activated when it becomes energized. It is only used for emergency situations."

"I see," Professor Willhaus replied. "I'm not opposed to being fitted with this device."

"Very well, I shall just be a moment," Professor Peabody said as he stood to retrieve the device. When he returned from his study he had what looked like a thin, wide strip of black strapping that resembled a man's watchband.

"The device is programmed for you, Reggie," he said. "I'll need your left arm, please."

Professor Willhaus extended his left arm and Professor Peabody turned it so the bottom of his wrist was facing up. He placed the device on his wrist and secured it in place. Then he gently slid his finger over the device, causing lights to flash where his finger had touched. As quickly as the lights illuminated they also dimmed. Once the last light faded, Professor Peabody removed the device.

"That's it?" Professor Willhaus asked skeptically.

"That is it," Professor Peabody replied.

"Are you sure it worked, Alistair?" he asked again. "Because I didn't feel a thing, nor do I feel anything now."

"It worked," Professor Peabody said. "If you gently rub the inside of your wrist you'll be able to locate the device I just implanted."

Professor Willhaus felt the slightest lump just at the location Professor Peabody had indicated.

"You should be completely unaware of the device for the most part. If you ever need to activate the alert, you simply apply firm pressure until you hear and feel a pop or cracking sensation."

"Amazing!" Professor Willhaus said, impressed.

Just as they were settling back down in their seats, Millie and Ditty returned to the sitting room as well.

"You'll be staying across the hall from Professor Peabody," Millie said to Professor Willhaus. "It's close to the library and very quiet. I think you'll be quite comfortable there."

"You're so very kind," Professor Willhaus said. "Thank you. I'm sure I will be most comfortable."

"I've filled the wardrobe for you too. Let me know if you need anything else," Ditty said.

"Thank you so much. It's more than I expected," he answered truthfully.

They spent the rest of the evening enjoying coffee and easy conversation. Professor Willhaus had spent some time talking with Sy and found his company enjoyable. He was keen to see the gardens, and Sy was happy to have someone who shared his enthusiasm for horticulture. Millie worked on her knitting while Lauren and Lainey played rummy. Finally it was time to call it a night. They had a busy day ahead of them and they all needed to get some rest. Tomorrow would prove to be a very exciting day.

Chapter 11

Lauren and Lainey were already in the dining room when Professor Peabody and Professor Willhaus arrived. The girls were slathering their toasted bagels with whipped cream cheese and topping it with freshly smoked lox. This was truly one of their absolute favorite breakfasts.

"Professor Willhaus, I trust you slept well?" Aggie asked as she looked up from her own breakfast.

"I most certainly did!" Professor Willhaus replied. "It's amazing, but I usually suffer from bouts of insomnia. To say that last night was the best sleep I've had in years would not be an exaggeration."

"I'm very pleased to hear that," Aggie said, smiling. "I think it's safe to say that we can credit your restful night's sleep to Sy."

Professor Willhaus looked confused.

"You see, in addition to his remarkable abilities with all things botanical, he is also an energy healer," Aggie said, reading the puzzled look on Professor Willhaus' face. "Although it's not something he does consciously, his energy will always balance those around him. It's said that energy healers draw their strength from the earth, causing them to be stable and balanced. It would seem that is the case with Sy since he spends many hours outdoors and finds tending the gardens quite fulfilling."

"So by spending a pleasant evening of enjoyable conversation with Sy, my energy was balanced, causing me to sleep soundly and restfully all night long. Amazing!" Professor Willhaus mused. "Well then, I am grateful to you, Sy."

"It's my pleasure, mate," Sy replied happily. "Now sit down and have yourself some breakfast!"

Professor Willhaus filled a plate and sat beside Sy. He was grateful for the restful night's sleep he had enjoyed, but he also found his company very pleasing. They talked easily about their gardens and successful techniques they'd used. Sy was happy to share his morning with Professor Willhaus. They sipped coffee and spoke easily with one another as if they were brothers who hadn't seen each other for ages. The clock chimed on the mantel indicating it was getting late.

"As much as I'd like to spend the rest of the day strolling through these beautiful grounds and enjoying your company, I believe we have a very special item to retrieve," Professor Willhaus said to Sy.

"I'll be sorry to see you go," Sy said. "But what you're doing to help us is much appreciated, Professor. I think I can speak for all of us when I say how grateful we are for your help, and when this is all over, we'll raise a pint together."

"I'll gladly take you up on that offer!" Professor Willhaus said with a hearty smile. "Now, Alistair, what's our plan for today's adventure?"

"We should start by heading to Paradise Island," Professor Peabody said. "REA can give us a visual on the crystal pyramid. Once we have a visual, then Lauren can apperate us to that location. Lainey will have her force field functional and expand it to include the four of us. If all goes well we should be home before lunch."

"Lovely!" Professor Willhaus said, clearly enjoying the prospect of the upcoming adventure.

"Shall we head to the sitting room, if everyone is ready?" Professor Peabody asked.

"I'm ready," Lainey said confidently.

"Me too," Lauren added.

"Off we go then!" Professor Willhaus chimed in.

Chapter 12

They gathered in the sitting room and all but Professor Willhaus stood by the mantle.

"What are you doing?" Professor Willhaus asked, looking a bit puzzled.

"Oh, I forgot! You've not been to Paradise Island yet," Professor Peabody said, amused. "You will need to stand by the mantle when the transport device is activated in order to be captured in the transport process."

Quickly Professor Willhaus joined the group. Professor Peabody activated the transport device. In the blink of an eye, they were transported to Paradise Island. Professor Willhaus tried to take everything in as quickly as he could. This was one of the most exciting things he had ever been involved in.

"Where are we exactly?" he asked.

"We are now on a cloaked island in the middle of the Pacific Ocean. It has never been mapped because it was cloaked prior to this region being charted," Professor Peabody patiently explained. "It's pretty amazing, don't you agree?" he asked, seeing the fascinated look on Professor Willhaus' face.

"Amazing doesn't even begin to cover it!" Professor Willhaus replied, awestruck.

Professor Peabody smiled. He enjoyed watching the many changing expressions cross Professor Willhaus' face while he experienced their world. They had a lot to share with each other.

"REA?" Professor Peabody called. "I wonder if you could assist us. We need a visual of the crystal pyramid of Atlantis, near the Tongue of the Ocean."

"There are three crystal pyramids in the location you requested. Please be more specific," REA answered in her smooth voice.

Surprise registered on everyone's faces. The fact that there was one confirmed sighting of a crystal pyramid in the Atlantic Ocean was amazing, but to discover that there were actually three structures meeting the criteria in that location was simply inconceivable. To think that the ancient ruins of Atlantis were still intact at the bottom of the ocean waiting to be discovered was beyond thrilling.

"I believe it's safe to say that we were not expecting that," Professor Peabody said, looking around at the other startled faces. "I expect we'll need a visual on all three, please."

Instantly three holographic screens appeared, two files layered behind the first. The first screen showed an image that was dark and obscured. The detail was very difficult to make out.

"I wonder if we could clean that image up a bit, please?" Professor Peabody asked. Instantly the image became clearer and in sharp focus. What they saw was mostly rubble. Apparently this crystal pyramid had collapsed and fallen in on itself, presumably when Atlantis sank. The crystals were covered in silt. Sea life had taken over most of the crystals, yet some of the blocks were still clear, as if the smoothness of the surface shed whatever tried to take hold.

"I don't believe this is the pyramid we've been looking for," Professor Peabody said. He touched the holographic image and pulled the next file forward. This image showed a fully intact crystal pyramid that seemed to be glowing as if the lights inside had been left on. The image was clear and crisp.

A few gasps could be heard. What they saw before them was breathtaking. The building, although in the shape of a traditional pyramid, was made entirely of crystal. There was depth and texture to the exterior that was completely unexpected. But the soft glow of light emanating from it was what made it so amazing. It stood so elegant and proud. Fish could be seen swimming around the exterior, giving the impression of calmness and serenity.

"Amazing!" Professor Willhaus muttered, gazing transfixed at the image. "The technology of the Atlantians is still considered superior to what we have in this so-called modern day." Turning to Professor Peabody he said, "Although I believe you could give them a run for their money, Alistair."

Professor Peabody smiled. "I believe you give us too much credit. Atlantians were a very advanced civilization. Unfortunately the accounts of their development were recorded by individuals whose knowledge of technology was primitive at best. Details and specifics are sadly lacking. Until there is the ability and the interest of excavating artifacts from the sea floor, I'm afraid the technology will remain lost. But now we shall concentrate on what we have come for. REA, could we see the interior image of this pyramid, please?"

The screen refreshed, and the image showed the interior of the pyramid. It was just as Professor Willhaus had described earlier. There was a huge rod suspended from the point in the ceiling and an enormous red jewel situated at the tip. It hovered about three feet above a pedestal with a set of shiny metallic hands situated on top. There was no sign of algae or crustaceans within the pyramid. It was pristine, as if it had just been cleaned. This pyramid looked so different from the first one.

"It looks exactly as I had imagined it. Just as the good doctor described it," Professor Willhaus said, astonished.

"This is really incredible!" Lainey cried. "Is this what you guys did when you found the first portal key?"

The others had been on the first portal key quest together. This was Lainey's first quest and she was certainly enjoying the mystery and thrill of the treasure hunt.

"It's so exciting to see something that hasn't seen the light of day in thousands of years, and presumably only one other modern day human being has actually touched it," Lainey continued. "It's unbelievable!"

"You have the makings of a world-class archeologist," Professor Willhaus said admiringly. "You have a passion for finding answers to the past. That is a skill that cannot be taught, it must be felt."

Lainey beamed.

"This is the fun part!" Professor Willhaus said as he rubbed his hands together. "Shall we?"

"I couldn't agree more." Lainey said happily as she extended her hand to Lauren.

"We could," Professor Peabody cut in. "But it may be wise to view the last remaining image before we depart."

Reluctantly Lainey lowered her hand and nodded in agreement even though she was anxious to get started. Professor Peabody touched the holographic image once more and pulled the next file forward. This image showed a second fully intact crystal pyramid identical to the one they'd just seen.

"REA, could we see the interior image of this pyramid as well?"

"Why it's an exact duplicate of the other one!" Professor Willhaus said incredulously as the image appeared.

"Indeed." Professor Peabody said touching the screen once more to place both images side by side.

"I say we go to this one first!" Lainey said pointing to the original image.

"Well then, shall we go and investigate this site?" Professor Peabody suggested.

He extended his hands to Lauren and Professor Willhaus. Lainey took Professor Willhaus' and Lauren's other hand as they formed a circle.

"Lainey, we shall need a force field to encompass just us for now. I will ask you to push it out when we get there," Professor Peabody instructed. "Can you do that?" Lainey nodded, and a force field surrounded them.

"Lauren, whenever you are ready," Professor Peabody said, turning to Lauren.

Lauren closed her eyes and concentrated on the crystal pyramid she'd just seen on the screen REA had provided. Although she was extraordinarily good at apperating, she wasn't sure she'd managed it because everything felt the same. She opened her eyes, half expecting to be disappointed. But she was surprised to find that they were inside the crystal pyramid. Lainey's force field was working perfectly.

"Way to go!" Lauren beamed at her sister. "I knew you could do it!"

"Nicely done, ladies," Professor Peabody said. "Alright, Lainey, push it out to the wall, please."

Lainey furrowed her brow and pushed the force field out with her mind. It was like watching her blow up a balloon. Slowly and gently it expanded until it engulfed the whole pyramid. When she was finished she seemed very pleased with herself.

She looked at Lauren and saw that she was smiling at her.

"Nice job, sis!" Lauren said clearly proud of her sister.

"Indeed," Professor Willhaus said in agreement. He began surveying his surroundings. He moved to the edge of the pyramid and touched the wall. He was surprised to feel how smooth it was; the seams were nearly indiscernible. The walls were cool and damp like the glass blocks in his shower back home. Although he could see the movement of fish outside the pyramid, he was unable to see the detail. It was surprising how calming the effect was. Then he turned and walked toward the middle of the room. He reached the center and carefully touched the metallic rod suspended from the tip of the pyramid. Attached to the end was an enormous, clear red gem that looked like a ruby. He allowed his fingers to gently touch the gem. The facets were cut in such a way that energy would be directed and contained within the hands below. His eyes followed the path to the shiny metallic hands. Something was wrong. His brow furrowed and he cocked his head to the side. He stroked his chin with the hand that had just touched the ruby.

"This is the wrong pyramid," he announced a little more loudly than he intended as his voice boomed unexpectedly off of the crystal walls.

Chapter 13

Everyone jumped as the sound of his voice broke the silence. They were surprised by the certainty of his declaration.

"How can you be so certain, Reggie?" Professor Peabody asked curiously.

"Because there is a large crystal sphere nestled in the hands. This cannot be the pyramid found by the doctor, because he confessed to removing the crystal sphere and taking it with him when he left," Professor Willhaus explained.

Professor Peabody turned to the south wall of the pyramid and scanned it for any anomaly within the crystal blocks. None could be found.

"I believe you're correct, Reggie. Although the crystal isn't transparent, I'm able to see well enough to note that there are no irregularities or variances concealed within the crystal," Professor Peabody agreed.

"We still have one more pyramid to explore," Lainey offered optimistically.

"True," Professor Peabody said. "Alright, ladies, shall we try it again?"

They all held hands, forming a circle, and Lainey pulled her force field in around them. Lauren then closed her eyes and apperated them to their final target. Once more they found themselves inside a self-illuminated crystal pyramid. Lainey pushed her force field out to allow free access to the entire pyramid. It was cool and damp inside, just as the previous pyramid had been. It smelled briny and fresh just as it does when one is near the ocean. This time they all walked directly to the altar and looked at the hands first. Relief swept over each of them as they realized the hands were empty. Unlike the previous crystal pyramid, this pyramid had been explored.

"I think we may have found it," Professor Peabody said, pleased. This time he went straight for the wall and located a dark irregularity within one of the crystal blocks. They all watched intently as he carefully inserted his hand into the crystal block, grasped an object, and slowly removed it from its resting place. When his hand finally came free of the crystal block, he opened it to reveal the shiny metallic portal key. It looked exactly as the two others had before it.

However, this was the first time Lainey had actually seen a portal key. Carefully she approached Professor Peabody and gently took the portal key from his hand. The portal key was small, about the size of a lemon, with a shiny metallic skin. It was star shaped and much heavier than its size would indicate, suggesting that the interior was solid, not hollow. She held it for a moment then handed it back to Professor Peabody. Professor Willhaus held his hand out next, and Professor Peabody placed the key in his hand. "It's awe-inspiring to hold something in one's hand that is from not only another world, but another galaxy. From a civilization that is no longer part of our existence. Human hands crafted this device and filled it with technology that we don't yet understand. It was intentionally placed here for safekeeping for us to find," Professor Willhaus said, uttering aloud what everyone else had been thinking. They noticed that Lainey was becoming anxious.

"Lainey, are you alright?" Professor Peabody asked.

"I know this is going to sound strange," Lainey said, "but when we're in the pyramid, I can almost feel an energy pulse on my force field. When I held the portal key, I felt the same thing in my hand only to a lesser degree."

"It doesn't sound strange at all," Professor Willhaus said. "If my theory is correct, these pyramids were designed to capture energy from various power sources including solar flares, celestial plasma showers, planetary tidal pulls, and even quasars, as impossible as that is to imagine. Atlantians sophisticatedly managed to harness these challenging energy sources, which we haven't even begun to consider. The pyramids would capture and store the energy until it was called for, then the pulse would be transmitted throughout the energy grid system. Imagine a never-ending clean energy source that relies on more than just one energy type to sustain life. I envision the crystal pyramids system was strategically placed to ensure maximum coverage. I also believe that depending on the moon's orbit as well as the position of Earth at any particular time of year, some pyramids may function at greater capacity than others. Gathering and storing energy and dispersing it to other pyramids within the grid system, ensuring constant, uninterrupted, stable energy. If you're feeling an energy pulse from the portal key, I suspect that the center of the portal key contains a pure form of crystal. As I understand it, the Atlantians were able to grow crystals very much like we grow tomatoes today."

"You're absolutely right, Reggie," Professor Peabody interjected enthusiastically. "Most advanced civilizations that we're familiar with grow crystals. It's a necessity. The people of Earth will never achieve true space exploration until they master crystal technology. The use of fossil fuel restricts the distance they can travel, while crystals hold unimaginable amounts of stable energy. Additionally, rocket fuel is extraordinarily unstable, while crystals are not. Finally, crystal energy can be recharged while en route. Since rocket fuel is consumed, it is not an energy source that can be replenished. Clearly crystal technology has many advantages."

"Uh...I really think we should go back now," Lainey said as her anxiety began to increase. "The pulse on my force field seems to be getting stronger."

"The energy build up may be getting ready to discharge," Professor Willhaus observed. "I agree. This may be a good time to head back."

They quickly formed a circle and held hands. Lauren closed her eyes and concentrated on Paradise Island. When she opened her eyes they were back in the sitting room. Lainey looked noticeably relieved. The holographic image still showed the interior of the crystal pyramid.

"Look at that!" Lauren said as she pointed to the image.

They saw that the rod suspended from the ceiling had begun to vibrate and the ruby-colored gem had started to glow. In an instant the most intense blue-green light shot from the tip of the gem directly into the palm of the brass-colored hands. The bolt of light crackled and danced but never strayed from its path directly into the center of the hands.

"Amazing," Professor Willhaus mused. "It looks just like a bolt of lightning."

The energy surge went on for nearly thirty seconds. When it finally stopped the brass hands were red hot and glowing but the rest of the pyramid seemed unaffected by the discharge.

"That might explain why there aren't any fish inside that thing!" Lainey said anxiously.

"I don't believe we were in any real danger," Professor Peabody said. "We had the protection of your force field, remember? The pulse you felt was more than likely the energy grid trying to equalize. It must have been unable to discharge while we were there…because of your force field."

"Do you still think apperating is better than force fields?" Lauren asked Lainey with a smirk on her face.

"I think I'll keep my force field," Lainey replied with a smile, feeling very pleased with herself.

Chapter 14

"It was certainly humbling to be inside the pyramid," Professor Willhaus said. "To think about Atlantis and how even a brilliant civilization such as that was no match for the forces of Mother Nature. Those pyramids were constructed over ten thousand years ago, and yet there they stand, fully intact and, amazingly, still functional. It's hard not to feel slightly overwhelmed. It makes one wonder what other treasures are still intact, waiting to be discovered."

"Yes, it does make one wonder, does it not?" Professor Peabody said as a twinkle crept into his eyes. "How marvelous it would be to do a little exploring and also how fortunate that we have a resource such as REA."

Professor Willhaus wasn't sure if Professor Peabody was toying with him. He searched Professor Peabody's face and felt certain that he was indeed thinking along the same lines as he was. Professor Willhaus could hardly contain his excitement.

"Alistair, are you suggesting what I hope you're suggesting?" Professor Willhaus asked in almost a pleading tone.

"I believe so," Professor Peabody said, smirking. "But first we should determine whether there are other Atlantian ruins that are as intact as the crystal pyramid."

"What are you two up to?" Lauren asked with a knowing smile.

Professor Peabody didn't answer her, but gave her a wink.

"REA, are there any other Atlantian locations that are relatively well preserved and safe for use to explore?" he asked.

"Affirmative," REA responded. "There are ninety-six locations created and used by the Atlantian race that are still identifiable."

"That many!" Lainey exclaimed, astounded.

"I wonder if we could get a visual of the top five locations, the first being the most intact?" Professor Willhaus asked.

"Certainly," REA answered. The image on the holographic monitor changed. They were now looking at an enormous courtyard the size of a football field. It was surrounded by what appeared to be villas. It had an enormous domed ceiling that extended far beyond the villas. It too seemed to be self-illuminating, and the domed ceiling was created of the same crystal blocks they had seen at the pyramid. Fish could be seen swimming lazily around statues and pillars. There were huge pots and planters that had once been home to enormous trees. Although the trees had long since faded, the frameworks of their trunks and branches could still be seen. The structure of branches had become home to various types of sea life. The image was spectacular. Brightly colored coral, sea anemones, and starfish created large, stunning underwater trees of pinks, purples, and blues. The center of the courtyard had what looked to be an enormous rectangular reflection pond. There were four large statues in the center, each in the process of emptying ornately carved clay jars. Clearly this would have been a spectacular water feature in the center of the square. All four statues had their backs pressed against an enormous pillar in the very center. The pillar rose high above the courtyard. Very little silt had worked its way into the center of the courtyard; however, unlike the crystal pyramid, they were unable to see anything but pitch black beyond the blocks.

"Would you ladies be interested in a little exploration of some ancient ruins of Atlantis?" Professor Peabody asked them with a grin.

"Would we ever!" Lainey said enthusiastically. She put up her force field and held out her hand to Lauren. They formed a circle, and Lauren took them there almost instantly. Her apperating skills were becoming stronger; she only needed to think about it now. Lainey started pushing her force field out so they could begin to explore the ruins, but as she did so she noticed the living trees struggling outside their watery home. Instantly her force field pulled back and the water returned to the trees. Her force field was no longer in the shape of a bubble but curved around the trees and other sea life. The courtyard was smattered with smaller bubbles filled with sea water.

"I didn't know you could do that!" Lauren said, astonished.

"I didn't know I could do that either!" Lainey said, just as surprised. "I just couldn't bear the thought of these gorgeous formations suffering because of me. As soon as I thought that, my force field pulled back and the water returned."

They walked to the edge of the water bubble and were surprised when their hands were able to penetrate Lainey's force field and touch the tree.

"Okay, that's really cool!" Lauren said, looking at Lainey.

"Yeah," Lainey agreed distractedly as she gently stroked a purple starfish while a school of little turquoise and black blue tang fish darted from one anemone to another. It looked like a beautiful fifteen-foot diameter aquarium that rose to the ceiling. Their eyes slowly followed the trunk up toward the ceiling. What they saw were the branches of the tree behind them intertwined with the one they were touching to create a canopy of living creatures. There were orange and white clown fish, hot pink wrasse, black and yellow triggers with spectacular white dots, and even neon blue damsel fish with their shocking yellow tails. It was breathtaking and oddly tranquil. Even thousands of years after Atlantis was lost, the beauty they created was still alive.

Their attention was drawn to the sound of Professor Peabody's voice off in the distance. "Amazing!" they heard him say. Reluctantly they drew their attention away from the living trees and walked toward the two professors in the middle of the courtyard. They were at the edge of the reflection pond directly in front of the four statues. In the image REA had provided, they hadn't notice the rod suspended in the middle of the dome that looked identical to the one they had seen in the crystal pyramid. However, the base in this application was shaped much differently. Tall and slender and made entirely of crystal, it rose up to meet the rod. Halfway up the crystal cylinder were what looked to be vents.

"This must be where the light source comes from," Professor Willhaus speculated. "The pyramid must send an energy pulse to locations like this. To think, they've left the lights on for over ten thousand years!"

They all laughed.

"But what are the vents for?" Lauren asked.

"I'm not certain," Professor Willhaus answered honestly.

"Look at this," Lainey said, indicating the statue to their left. "It's so lifelike."

"...And beautiful." Lauren observed dreamily.

Indeed; the statue was of an extraordinarily handsome young man with a crown perched atop his long, silky mane of hair, his hand outstretched toward another statue of a lovely young maiden. She too wore a crown atop her head with hair that flowed well down her back. Their eyes were locked, and it wasn't hard to imagine that they cared deeply for one another, and perhaps even belonged to each other.

"The crowns would indicate that this is a royal couple," Professor Willhaus said. "I suspect this was their home or perhaps even their kingdom. We know so little about Atlantis, but I believe this must be King Chronos. Presumably there were detailed accounts of Atlantis in the Royal Library of Alexandria. Unfortunately the library was destroyed in a fire during the time of the Roman Empire, specifically the reign of Julius Caesar. As unimaginable as it may seem, Caesar intentionally set the fire that eventually burned the library to the ground. True, the library was not his intended target, but the effect was all the same. The full impact of losing that ancient collection of literary treasures is still bitterly felt today."

"What exactly was the Royal Library of Alexandria?" Lainey inquired.

"It was called the Royal Library of Alexandria, but in truth it more resembled a university campus or an institution of higher learning," Professor Willhaus explained. "Apparently there were gardens and walking paths, dining halls, meeting and reading rooms, and even lecture halls. The exact arrangement of the facility is not known. However, what is known is that there were halls containing enormous shelves. Those shelves held vast collections of scrolls, since papyrus was the only existing method of book publishing at the time. The library was the first of its kind and came into existence primarily because of its location being in the most affluent and metropolitan city of its time. All trade from the east and west was funneled through Alexandria. It is said that any ship that made port in Alexandria was inspected for, and required to relinquish, every book on the vessel. The books would be expertly copied and the replica returned to the ship, as the original would be kept in the library. Additionally it is said that in later years Marc Antony pillaged and plundered other libraries and gifted nearly two hundred thousand scrolls to his beloved Cleopatra as a wedding gift. It is believed there were over half a million scrolls in Alexandria prior to the fires. The library's vast collections included books of mathematics, astronomy, physics, and other subjects."

"Julius Caesar burned it down?" Lainey asked incredulously.

"Sadly, yes," Professor Willhaus replied. "The details are sketchy, but the most accepted theory is that the fire was started at Caesar's command. He instructed his soldiers to burn the Egyptian navy, which had defiantly ported in Alexandria, but it quickly got out of hand and a firestorm ensued."

"It makes me so sick to think that someone would burn a library," Lauren said. "I don't understand how anyone could do that even if it was an accident."

"Power does strange things to people," Professor Peabody replied. "The Roman Empire ruled in complete unrestrained authority. Few dared to question them, and those who did, did so at their own peril and often with grave consequences. The absolute power that the emperors wielded must have been terrifying. No one person or group should ever have that kind of control over a civilization again."

The mood had turned somber. There was still more to explore, yet they were lost in thought and saddened by the tale of the Alexandrian library and the fate of the beautiful people of Atlantis.

"Perhaps we should head back," Professor Peabody suggested. They all solemnly agreed.

"I'd like to remember this place as tranquil and harmonious," Lauren said as she took one last look around her. She held out her hands, and they formed a circle while Lainey pulled her force field in tight around them. They watched as the water rushed in and the courtyard returned to the sea once more. Taking one last look around her, Lauren took them back to Paradise Island.

Chapter 15

"I hope one day we can go back to Atlantis," Lainey offered hopefully.

"I think we would all like that," Professor Willhaus agreed. "There are so many things I would like to explore in more detail. For instance, why were there vents on that pillar and..."

"The vents on the pillar were designed to cool the area beneath the dome," REA answered.

Startled, they all looked at one another. They had never imagined that REA would be able to answer their questions.

"REA, you never cease to amaze me," Professor Peabody said, chuckling.

"Cool the courtyard and villas?" Professor Willhaus asked, flabbergasted. "You mean like an air conditioner?"

"The concept of air conditioning is rudimentary, but yes, that is the correct idea," REA explained. "The location you have just returned from is near what is now known as the Canary Islands off the coast of Africa. The temperature can be uncomfortably warm for humans. The cooling system used by the Atlantians would have kept the living space quite comfortable."

"I have a question," Lainey asked. "There's something that's been bothering me since we've come back. Why were all the benches so large? Were they giants or something?"

"I think I might be able to answer that question," Professor Willhaus interjected. "REA, correct me if I'm wrong, but the people of Atlantis looked much different than the people of Earth do today. The Atlantians were beautifully tanned with manes of thick blonde hair and piercing blue eyes. However, the most striking feature was their height. The Atlantians were all over nine feet tall and could reach as high as twelve feet tall."

"That is correct," REA agreed.

"There is so much to learn about Atlantis," Lauren observed.

"But that will have to wait for another day," Professor Peabody said. "It's getting late and we still need to place the portal key we've retrieved today.

"Golly, I'd forgotten all about it!" Lainey replied.

"Well, I think we should see what we have here," Professor Peabody said. "REA, we would like to place the next portal key, please."

The portal key box appeared on the coffee table. Professor Peabody lifted the lid to reveal the inside of the ornate box. The interior was a familiar sight to Lauren and Professor Peabody. However, Professor Willhaus and Lainey had never seen it before. What they saw were nine indentations—presumably each would hold one of the portal keys. Two of the indentations already held a portal key that looked exactly like the portal key in Professor Peabody's hand. He placed the third key in the next position.

The box illuminated with a soft green glow and a voice said, "You have successfully retrieved the third portal key and placed it in the correct position. The fourth portal key is located in what is now known as the Canary Islands, specifically the island of Tenerife. On the east side of the island you will find the black pyramids constructed by the Guanches. The Guanches people are generally considered to be an extinct race. However, during the Spanish invasion of the 1500s several clans found refuge through the pyramids. The pyramids were sealed and the entrance obscured; the Spaniards never knew of their existence. Today, within that majestic mountain, the survivors of this magnificent race still thrive. The portal key has been secured within a frozen chamber at the center of the mountain. The 'Keepers' are the chosen few who have been safeguarding this ancient artifact, awaiting the day when the travelers return to claim it. In order to complete the quest, the seekers must possess the ability to thermally manipulate and phase cooperatively in order to retrieve the protected portal key. In addition you will also need this medallion to gain access to the hidden archway." The voice finished speaking and the box stopped glowing. Lying next to the box was a flat, round, shiny metallic medallion with a hole in the middle and a thin leather strap attached to it. Professor Willhaus picked up the medallion and began inspecting it as Lauren looked over his shoulder.

"Interesting, I've never seen metal like this before. I believe this is made of bronze, but in all honesty I'm not completely sure that's true. There's an inscription within the circle, but the letters are nothing I've ever seen before," he said, looking up. He handed the medallion to Professor Peabody.

"Well, you phase," Lauren said, "...but who thermally manipulates?"

Professor Peabody sighed deeply. "Well, that does present a problem, because I don't know of anyone who is a thermal manipulator." He handed the medallion to Lainey.

"What does 'thermally manipulates' mean exactly?" Professor Willhaus asked.

"Someone whose ability permits them to manipulate the kinetic energy of atoms, allowing them to generate as well as absorb heat or fire," Professor Peabody answered.

"I don't understand," Lainey said to Professor Peabody. "Why can't you just phase the portal key out of the frozen chamber just like you did with the crystal block?"

"That would certainly make things easier, my dear," Professor Peabody said. "But you see my ability to phase is limited to materials whose molecular characteristics fall within normal limits. The molecular characteristics of frozen liquid render my gift ineffective. That's why a thermal manipulator is necessary. I'm unclear as to how a thermal manipulator and phaser would work cooperatively together. In all honesty I didn't know it could be done. Very clever indeed," he said thoughtfully.

"I'll need to do some research on the ancient Guanches," Professor Willhaus stated. "I've been to Tenerife and studied the pyramids there on two occasions, but I never imagined there were hidden archways that allow one to gain internal access to Mount Teide. If that's the case, and this ancient civilization still exists..." He trailed off, deep in thought.

'What is it, Reggie?" Professor Peabody asked, tilting his head quizzically to one side.

"Alistair, the commonly accepted theory is that the ancient Guanches were survivors of Atlantis," Professor Willhaus said calmly, allowing the full impact of what he said to sink in. The two men stared at one other for a long moment as their minds raced. They were brought back to the present when Lauren spoke.

"If what you're saying is true, then we could actually meet someone from Atlantis?" she asked.

"Their decedents, yes," Professor Peabody said. "I think we had better return to Waverly Park. We should share what we have found with Aggie; perhaps she can shed some light on the subject."

"Great idea, I'm hungry," Lainey said. "We've missed lunch!"

Clearly, meeting the Guanches was going to have to wait until she'd had some dinner. They all laughed and headed to the mantel.

Chapter 16

The transport device was activated, and the party of four returned to the sitting room at Waverly Park. The clock began to chime, indicating that it was six o'clock in the evening.

"Is that the time?" Professor Peabody asked startled. "We've been gone much longer than I thought. We should get washed up and meet back in the dining room—on the double. Dinner is being served and you know how Ditty is if we're late."

They all quietly left the sitting room and darted upstairs to their rooms to get cleaned up. They met back in the corridor just outside the dining room. Apparently they felt there would be power in numbers. They took a deep breath and pushed Professor Peabody to the front. He gave them an annoyed look and then boldly opened the door and walked in with the rest of them following closely.

"We do apologize for being tardy, but it really could not be helped," he said with a winning smile. "Oh, Ditty, dinner smells divine." He took his seat, hoping she wasn't watching him. The others quietly took their seats as well. Lainey was the only one who made eye contact with Ditty. For some reason Lainey was always able to get away with more than the others.

"Aunt Ditty, you really have outdone yourself this time," Lainey said to her. "No one makes pasta like you!"

Sy raised an eyebrow and glanced sideways in Ditty's direction, careful not to let her see. Ditty was in a mood, but her expression began to soften when Lainey spoke to her.

"You're late," Ditty said with more concern in her tone now that her irritation had begun to fade.

"I know," Lainey said apologetically, "and we're really sorry."

"If I know you're here for dinner then I know you're safe for the evening. With everyone still missing, dinner's more important than ever," Ditty said with feeling.

Lainey got up and came around the table. She hugged Ditty tightly from the back and kissed her affectionately on the cheek.

"I'm sorry," Lainey said sincerely, "we'll try harder next time."

Sy smiled and shook his head, trying to suppress a chuckle as he continued eating. Lainey had always known how to pull Ditty out of her moods.

"Go on and sit now, child!" Ditty said. "Your dinner is getting cold."

Professor Peabody winked appreciatively at Lainey as she returned to her seat. They were all famished and started passing around the trays of pasta mounded with sauce. One tray was filled with spaghetti and meatballs, another with shrimp scampi full of fat pink prawns in a succulent garlic sauce. The final tray was filled with great slabs of fried eggplant covered in a thick layer of marinara and melted mozzarella cheese. A huge platter of Italian deli treats sat in the center of the table next to sliced crusty bread. The platter was filled with thin slices of salami, mortadella, capicolla, spicy pepperoni, fresh mozzarella, provolone, and a garlic ricotta spread that made everyone's mouth water. The salad was tossed with a wonderful vinaigrette, and the garlic bread was tender and warm. They ate enthusiastically and all had seconds. Professor Willhaus and Lainey had thirds.

"Oh, I'm so full I could just burst," Lainey complained when she finally put her fork down.

"Well now, that's a shame," Ditty said in mock disappointment, "because I have a nice warm batch of lemon bars just out of the oven."

"Lemon bars!" Professor Willhaus and Lainey said in unison as they sat up.

"I have room for lemon bars," Professor Willhaus said eagerly as everyone laughed.

Once they were comfortably situated in the sitting room with their coffee and lemon bars (of which Professor Willhaus had two), they began sharing the details of their most recent journey. How REA showed them not one but three crystal pyramids near the Tongue of the Ocean and how Lainey was able to feel the energy pulse on her force field. They told how they began to explore the ruins of Atlantis and of the statue of King Chronos and his bride and the beautiful aquatic tree filled with the most amazing creatures. Then they explained how little was known about Atlantis because of the fires at the Royal Library of Alexandria. Finally they told of placing the most recent portal key and the requirements of the next quest. Aggie could not think of one person who thermally manipulated and found it extraordinary that two gifts would need to be combined in order to perform the quest requirements.

It was a lovely evening with wonderful food and wonderful company. The weather was turning cold, and the fall colors could be seen in the garden from the sitting room windows. Bowser and Bosco snored lazily by the crackling fire as the evening wore on. Finally it was time to say goodbye to their friend Professor Willhaus.

"Lauren and Millie should accompany you on your return home," Professor Peabody explained to Professor Willhaus. "Millie's gift of invisibility should ensure your arrival goes unnoticed."

"Capital idea, Alistair," Professor Willhaus agreed. "I certainly would not want to try and explain my sudden appearance. I can only imagine what difficulties that would cause me," he said, chuckling.

"We shall do our best to resolve the 'thermal manipulation' issue," Professor Peabody said, "while you try to find out as much as you can about the ancient Guanches."

"I'm on the case!" Professor Willhaus said with high spirits. "As difficult as it may be, I'll try to keep from being startled the next time you 'pop' into my library unexpectedly."

"But that's part of the fun," Lauren said, smiling.

They all said their farewells. It was becoming more difficult to see Professor Willhaus return to his life away from Waverly Park. They had become so fond of him and enjoyed his company immensely.

"It's been a pleasure, sir," Sy said, stepping forward and extending his hand to Professor Willhaus. "I do look forward to spending more time with you."

"And I with you, my friend," Professor Willhaus said honestly as he shook Sy's hand. "I'm so pleased to have found a companion whose interests are so like my own. I look forward to wandering your gardens with you."

Chapter 17

Lauren extended her hands to Millie and Professor Willhaus.

"Until next time..." Professor Willhaus said, and then they were gone.

It was a good thing they had brought Millie with them because when they arrived in Professor Willhaus' library, two of his younger colleagues were standing near his desk discussing his absences with his secretary.

"You're telling me that you haven't seen him for two days!" the taller of the two colleagues said incredulously.

"It's not unlike him to take some time to clear his head," Professor Willhaus' secretary explained, sounding a bit rattled. "He's a brilliant man. Brilliant men can be eccentric at times."

"You're not grasping the full impact," the short, round colleague said. "He has access to valuable and sensitive documents. Documents that should be safeguarded at the very least and certainly kept from general viewing if at all possible! If he is *missing time*, so to speak, then his mental faculties could be in question."

"I wouldn't say he's *missing time* exactly," the secretary argued. "He just leaves for a few days. He always comes back, and I don't think his 'mental faculties' are in question!"

"I don't think you're qualified to make that determination," the tall colleague said coolly. With that the two young colleagues glanced at one another with arrogant smiles and left the secretary alone in the library.

"Oh, Professor Willhaus!" the secretary said in aggravation to the empty office. "Those two are bound to make trouble for you, and you're not helping yourself!" She turned the light off in his office and closed the door behind her as she left. Once the door closed Professor Willhaus and his two companions appeared.

"Who were those two men?" Lauren asked a bit irritated.

"Those boys are nothing to worry about," Professor Willhaus said, unaffected. "But I do believe I should increase Lillian's salary, or at the very least give her a nice little bonus for having to deal with those pompous windbags."

Professor Willhaus' explanation alleviated their concern. Lauren and Millie grinned then gave Professor Willhaus a hug and said good-bye. They held hands and disappeared, leaving him standing in the center of his dark library.

Professor Peabody, Aggie, and Lainey were still up waiting for them when they returned.

"No trouble, I assume?" Professor Peabody inquired.

Lauren explained what they had witnessed and how Professor Willhaus had dismissed the intrusion as trivial.

"Well, if Reggie has no concerns then I think we should respect that," Professor Peabody said.

"I know," Lauren said, "I just have this uncomfortable feeling about it. Professor Willhaus is such an amazing man and it makes me mad that people treat him badly. Those two men gave off a really bad energy signature."

"You can read energy signatures?" Lainey asked, amazed.

"Yeah, that's how I can apperate to a person as well as a location," Lauren explained.

"Is it like an aura?" Lainey asked, fascinated.

"I hadn't thought of it like that, but I guess so," Lauren answered thoughtfully. "Even though I don't see colors, I can tell moods. Everyone has an energy signature, and we all read it to a certain extent, I'm just really good at it."

"I'd love to sit and chat with you all about this, but I'm pooped," Millie said. "I'm going to bed!"

Thunder cracked and rain began pelting the windows on the French doors. Bowser lifted his head to see where Lauren was and then laid it down again. Bosco yawned and stretched, then moved a little closer to the dying embers of the fire in the grate.

"That's not a bad idea, Millie," Aggie said. "I think we should all call it a night. Tomorrow we shall try to figure out how on earth we can find a thermal manipulator—no pun intended."

Chapter 18

Lauren lay awake in her dark room listening to the thunder boom off in the distance. The rain pelted her window as the howling wind bent the trees, causing them to protest with angry groans and creaks. The lightning cracked once again, illuminating the blustering leaves and whipping trees outside her bedroom window. Bosco the Boston snored contentedly, completely unaffected by the tempest that was brewing beyond the warmth and safety of his mistress's bedroom. Lauren, on the other hand, couldn't sleep. She'd seen blustery storms like this before, and actually found them almost thrilling, but for some reason tonight she just couldn't shake the feeling that something was wrong. She tried in vain but couldn't put her finger on it. She knew that something other than the storm was bothering her, but what? She rolled over in bed and pulled the covers close to her chin as another clap of thunder struck. She closed her eyes, trying to clear her mind, and waited for sleep to come. It was going to be a long night.

www.ingramcontent.com/pod-product-compliance
Lightning Source LLC
Chambersburg PA
CBHW031652040426
42453CB00006B/284